SOMETHING BRIGHT, THEN HOLES

MAGGIE NELSON

SOFT SKULL PRESS

BROOKLYN NY, 2007

Something Bright, Then Holes
© 2007 Maggie Nelson
ISBN 13: 978-1-933368-80-1

Interior design by Kimi Traube
Cover design by Nora Nussbaum
Cover art: "Heartattack City" by Tara Jane O'Neil

Published by Soft Skull Press
55 Washington St, Suite 804
Brooklyn NY 11021

Distributed by Publishers Group West
www.pgw.com

Library of Congress Cataloging-in-Publication Data
available from the Library of Congress

CONTENTS

SOMETHING BRIGHT, THEN HOLES

I used to do this, the self I was
used to do this

the selves I no longer am
nor understand.

Something bright, then holes
is how a girl, newly-sighted, once

described a hand. I reread
your letters, and remember

correctly: you wanted to eat
through me. Then fall asleep

with your tongue against
an organ, quiet enough

to hear it kick. Learn everything
there is to know

about loving someone
then walk away, coolly

I'm not ashamed
Love is large and monstrous

Never again will I be so blind, so ungenerous
O bright snatches of flesh, blue

and pink, then four dark furrows, four
funnels, leading into an infinite ditch

The heart, too, is porous;
I lost the water you poured into it

THE CANAL DIARIES

The Canal Sitters

Every evening the canal sitters
make their way down the street, past

the gigantic mustard-colored pipes
that grind up cement, past

the pale blue and pink factories
exhaling through their vents

Past the marble warehouse with its vats of stucco
Past the oil trucks that stain the walls of their stable

Past the yellow diamond that reads DEAD END
then farther down, another: END

It's why we've come here, apparently, and why
we already know we may not stay long

Meanwhile the sitters have lived here forever
Their job is to sit and watch for new life

Sit and see if anything is growing, has grown, will grow
Sit and see what life is left after all human attempts

to strangle it. What could possibly be born.
They sit and watch the cliffs, they sit and watch

the water. They sit and watch the pigeons
wheel above the cement crusher's

mean lavender dust. You have to watch
very carefully. You have to sit at dusk

with the man who wears all black, with his
white beard, his ropey face. You cannot ask

his name. You have to use
a quiet pen. You have to notice

the white moth on the engorged
gladiola, you have to pay attention

to the wind. You have to go inside
if the wind moves the dust toward you

And it may come flying toward you
Invisible, coarse, and possible

Flying like a knife down the water.

*

Green

Screams from an Italian family up the street
That stupid kid hitting rock after rock with his metal bat.

I'd be a shitty boyfriend, you said, as if
making a promise. I said, *It's not the content*

I'm in love with, it's the form. And that
was tenderness. All last year

I planned to write a book about
the color blue. Now I'm suddenly surrounded

by green, green gagging me
pleasurably, green holding onto my hips

from behind, digging into
the cleft, the cleft

that can be made. You have no idea
what kind of light you'll let in

when you drop the bowl, no idea
what will make you full

*

One week

One week on the canal, one week
of this new life. Each day brings
astonishing sights; each day
I'm more petrified.

Maybe living with you doesn't have to be so hard
(not a new thought)

If I could uproot the weed in me
the weed that grows and grows
so rank and garrulous, so greedy
for the sun, its supremacy

In the library I pick up book after book of poetry

All of the voices are up late, sticky
in their pajamas, all of them are listening
to imaginary foxes, sounding out their cells
and writing the distance down.

*

The man in black

The man I feared most
is now the man with whom I sit
at every sunset.

I didn't know

*

The Collector

Early evening, a guy with a shopping cart full of debris.
He speaks in a raspy whisper, so if you want to hear him
you have to get very close to his mouth.

They dump down here at night, he says. *Always have. Pure*
economics. They pay a guy like me 50 bucks
to come dump. But I don't dump, he says.
I collect, he says.

*

A Desk in the Weeds

The dumping makes me angry.
This week, a desk in the weeds, all the drawers
locked shut. Used condoms stuck
to the faux wood like slugs.

Then one morning all the drawers
were pried open, but there were no hidden
treasures, just an old lady's datebook,
old lady handwriting.

Fell asleep in the East Broadway subway station last night
until the Mobile Washing Unit spilled water mixed with bleach
on my feet, as if I were just some sludge
that came with the station, which, in a sense,

I was. Now it's a new day, full of promises
I can't keep, or am choosing to be unable.

*

Invisible

Last night I made a pact
with the man
in black. His hands
were rough

*

Special water

Low tide, a little girl picks up a stone
and puts it in her mouth; her father yells *NO*
and peels it out. *This is special water*

he says, gently shaking her
little body. *It may look pretty
but it's very, very bad for you.*

The dog doesn't care, she prances
in the muck, then climbs in my lap
and licks. *Some habits die hard,* says her owner

His wet black blunt smelling like heaven

*

Night-sitting

Went down to the canal last night
at one a.m., my first time
night-sitting. The water was black or just
the darkest green, ultra-perilous
its slow lapping bringing back
my old impulse to suicide
suddenly, without being
unhappy, or at least without
knowing it. Last night before we hung up
I called you *my friend.* It felt right, for
the moment. The green canoe still humps
the red canoe, the water very still
though the trees are shaking, the fish monitors
just tired logs and nets, bobbing stupidly
against the cliff. You said my last letter
takes up a lot of space; is radiant.
I do feel a light growing, from far inside,
like the moon just a bit fatter

than half. And now after one sitting
I'm no longer scared of the canal at night
Not scared to sit on the concrete slab
stained with graffiti, not afraid to admire
the new rash of marigolds
glowing in the white, industrial light.

*

Raccoon Watch

What's new? I ask the man in black.
One blue heron, he says, *but it didn't land.*

He doesn't want to talk, doesn't look
in my direction. *I'm on raccoon watch,* he explains.

Forty silent minutes later, three raccoons
come out of their burrows, braid their bodies

along the cliff. *It'll be raccoon stew tonight
for the homeless!* he cries, clapping his hands

together, as the moon rises gold
behind them, another goddamn sign

*

All the parts

We're going to get sprinkles, he says.
We're going to get thunder.

I sit on my notebook, ready
to keep it dry. First light, then harder

the drops make an orgy of circles
on the water. *Only I can save*

myself, you said, a knowledge
that goes both ways. Where the drops hit

the paper, pale red spots appear
Some deep chemical mystery

All the parts I failed to cover

*

Reckless

When the rain comes
the water lifts itself up

and surpasses the moss
line, oozes over

the cobblestones,
threatening everything

in its path. Last night
I dreamt I didn't move

in time, just stepped in
Totally unmindful

Totally reckless
My feet thus lost

to the live virus

*

27 Days of Rain

Is it action that waits
in the wings of
emotion, or

is this feeling
all that will remain?
Actual touch is

overrated, some say.
I differ. Go to sleep
in anger and heat

and wake again
to the pour
of rain, streets

emptied of their
carnival. Pink prints
on white tissue

announce another month's
passing, inconsolable.
Who's to say

if this whirring
is predestined
yearning, or simply

the otter grown tired
of playing its harp
on one side? I couldn't

chisel anything more
off my life, not even
if I tried.

*

Night Herons

There are rumors
of night herons

Red eyes
Yellow legs

I'll believe it
when I see it

All I've seen
are those long, blonde bodies

that race along the surface
at night, fast as bats

but fat with grace
and power.

*

Twinned
                    for BB

It's good to see you, you
who shows me the salt boxes

on the bridge, you who
will sit with me late

at the edge. The water
is perfectly still, as if

we pressed the planet
on pause, the trees and factories

reflected so precisely
that no horizon is

possible. The world thus
appears as it truly is:

twinned, or twice
as deep and large.

*

That rusty door

The barbed wire is lovely tonight
and the sparrows don't mind
its tangle. How many ways are there

to get saturated in another's mind?
I play my little movie of you
over again, trying to discover

any lost details. When I open my eyes
I see that rusty door across the canal
that leads from nowhere to nothing, just like

that Cuban prison, where the poet
stumbles out of the sump
and God is waiting with his freedom

*

Which cloud

As summer thickens the garden gets
explosive, almost angry: tall, weepy
coils, psychotic
vegetables. You could break
a hard-won sobriety
just by looking at it. Look
somewhere else, for God's sake,
look up. Which cloud
does God live on? *The one*
in the foreground, the gold one, the one
by all the mottled blue. In the morning

when we could finally see
you said you were trying to understand
my face. *Or maybe it's
the marbled one, the one that looks like Earth
as seen from outer space*

*

Lonelyville

The afternoon sun comes & puts
its shadows on the wood

A blue hump for my hand
A sharp dark curl for a stalk

The water here runs thin and sweet with rust
I will fly toward you, if I must

*

Evensong

Giving up? the man asks
when I close my book

Yes, the light is fading

I know I could read your poems
in the dark, but I am allowed only one

a day, and even that's
too much.

*

The Ides of July

Lost in time, wind coming in
from the wrong direction. There are men

who control the bridges from sealed
yellow chambers, they stay up all night

and guard the river. *You're just picking at it
like a scab*, it's the kind of thing

someone's mother would say, probably mine.
The wind starts in the tree that's greediest

for possession, then moves on to seize
the whole stand. Someone tied a sweatsock

round a loop of barbed wire. Someone lost
their Levis in the water. I'm jumpy tonight,

keep thinking someone's in the bushes
A dumper, a looter, a squatter, a mugger

He writes like a spider got hold of a pen, it's that wild.
The lower rung of sky is washed in pink

but the magic that slapped me awake
has momentarily chosen to abate, my antennae

wilted, no shoulder missing my head.
YOU SUCK STAG BALLS it says

on a rowboat's back. A phantom orchestra strikes up
from the abandoned brick palace

which supposedly houses magnificent ballrooms
but the whole lot is toxic. In the ides of July,

it's suddenly quite cold, Canadian air
chilling each spot I've sweat. One by one

the floodlights wink on, abolishing
night, soon all the colors will be illumined

by artificial light, thus separating us from
our ancestors. Now a woman appears

beside me, she has good-smelling coffee,
sandals, binoculars, says she wants to see

the raccoons. No one has seen them for days.
The fireflies have dried up too, so the kids

have been bringing their own in jars.
You're robbing this of joy, you tell me

as if I were the thief, as if
I had the goods in hand.

*

The summer before the summer

I don't feel like going down
to the canal today. The summer's

halfway through, and already
over. *No more words*

from the field! Thus begins
the slow slide back

to my life, back
to the plans I drew

before the summer
became the summer

of wanting you

*

These days

Last night a stranger called
at 2 a.m., said, THE CODE WORD
IS *SHOES*. If only it were

that easy. I get so happy
when I think that you
exist, it's this creepy

euphoria, the other night
I felt so high, one of
the bar regulars brought me

a cardboard box from
the dumpster, so I could
break dance, blow off

some steam. I hear
they have to shut off
one of the canal's

propellers, probably this
winter, so that the stench
doesn't come up. I don't see

why they don't just fix it
instead of leaving the water
to rot. Yet I know

it's so much work
to dredge it, to face a century
of muck. These days

the world seems to split up
into those who need to dredge
and those who shrug their shoulders

and say, *It's just something
that happened.* A century ago
there was a Miss Gowanus

contest here, a woman
with a sash on a barge. Now
there's a metal railing

so that people don't dump
their cars. *Our talks somehow*
settle my heart, you said. Me too.

Though how can it be, as
my heart has become so unsettled
by you. But I trust you

to take care of
yourself, and in a sense
that's all that matters. And

I, too, am finally learning
something similar, how
to protect the spirit's grandeur.

*

37 days

after work I stumble down to the edge, unable to resist
the lure. 37 days since I found you and lost you, 37 days
of feeling lost and found. I don't want to be writing
these poems into winter, the outline of your cock
still etched in my brain, all new life hiding or dying
as the canal chokes with ice. for now it's still summer,
the red lights on the drawbridge making wavy red slits
on the water, bringing a strange sort of peace, until a car
comes careening down the block with its headlights off
and two guys jump out to piss. then I'm just another girl
in a dress, a roll of twenties in her pocket, risking it.

*

Another night falls

It's been hot, the violets
are tired. The daisies

are peeling, and my whole hand
is shaking. Two Rastas

have parked at the edge to play
loud music, but even they

can't compete with the wind.
One heart, so many different

truths. As if on cue, the man in black
arrives, this time on a bike. He's so old,

I didn't know he could ride. But really
he can do anything. My desire is so

fierce, I came down to air it out
and still I feel it shred the space

around me. Tomorrow I will paint
another spot of oil on my sternum

for clarity. *You always put the cart
before the horse*, you tell me.

It's the promise that has to come first.
You may be right, or that may be right

for you, but I have to stay down
here, I have to watch the yellow leaves

float on the surface, spinning in
the constant wind. Queen Anne's lace

graces the banks, sunflowers
climb the aluminum wall, the Rastas

move on. There is a truth that
I'm going for, but I can only sketch

its contours. God knows
I am still waiting for an answer.

*

"What is it?"

A sad dusk here, the water
swollen with debris.

The blue wrapper of an Almond Joy;
the hourglass of a Maxi.

Some of the garbage sinks, inexplicably
but most of it just floats by

A bag of Lay's, another Maxi.
Today the man in black wears

glasses; I wonder how much
one has to drink to achieve

that nose. Yet I get the feeling
he doesn't drink anymore.

He greets a filthy dog brought
by a skinny hippie. The dog's teeth

are blood-stained, his hair
falling out in clumps. *He doesn't*

really know what he wants, the hippie says
as his dog sniffs the water.

Join the club, says the man in black.
The hippie tells us his dog

has terrible luck. A week ago
it fell into a silo; yesterday

it got electrocuted while peeing
on a pole. We don't really know

how to respond. The sky is amazing
tonight, full of blurry swans.

Why should I keep writing you? I ask.
Because there's a purity in it. And so

there is. When the hippie finally leaves,
the man in black whispers to me:

*It walks like a parrot, is scrawny,
fishes, and has dark legs. What is it?*

How the hell should I know?
I'm living a lie.

*

All Those
              for JR

I charge myself with
impatience, chicanery
then call you for
the diagnosis

You say it's just the spirit
looking out for its own
vastness, yes
But still I envy

all those who are hungry
and get fed, all those
who still use recreational drugs
Those happy & fat with child

Those who tell the truth
and delight in it, those who believe
in a compassionate
wilderness, those

whose bodies beget
an absolute forgetfulness.
Have you ever met
one of those people

who can pick out any tune
on any instrument, then
fill the night with sound?

*

Today's storm

After we talked, the rain came down
in torrents, rushing down

the cobblestones, all forces
breakneck to the water. Nothing

could stop it. The man in black
stood at the edge, sporting

a poncho, asked me
if I had come for a dip. I said

I was already wet, and
how true. Though today

I felt it: you don't want me
as much as I want you.

Sad, as they say, but true.
Still you like to hear me

say it, so I'll tell you again:
I want you. I want you.

It's a relief to be bereft
of shame, of guilt, to know

what you want. To want.
And if you don't want me

there is still no shame, only
white legs of lightning,

thunder.

*

"A Somber Poem"

The lowest tide I've yet seen
A giant blue crab hangs

from a chrome shopping cart
on the canal floor, the depths

suddenly visible. They say
a gang of homeless teens

has set up camp
in the cliff; now a curious rope

dangles from the cement
carcasses. A college kid

is growing sea grasses
in floating boxes, the desk in the weeds

has been completely hacked
up, just another piece of junk

along with the umbrellas
and wildflowers. At dusk

a canal-sitter brings me a sheaf
of his poems. They have

amazing titles, like "Big on Pig,"
"A Somber Poem," and

"The Savior of Sour."
I promise to return

the favor. The sky moves
from gray to yellow to blue

and I am missing you in the way
that spreads. I'm trying

to wear my freedom like
an amulet, make it something

I'll never forget.

*

The Birder

I know the birder is here
before I see him, he leaves

the soft leather case
for his binoculars

on the cement slab, then
climbs over to perch

atop the rowboat's back.
See that small white rectangle

across the canal? he asks.
I don't, but I nod.

This morning I packed three gigantic
peanut butter sandwiches, then took out

the red canoe. Planted the food
along the cliff, then watched all day

to see what would come eat it.
He says only one sandwich

is left; the others were eaten
by an opossum, or maybe just

a giant rat. *No birds*
today? I ask.

*

Seen it all

Just when you thought
you'd seen it all

A man stands by
the open passenger door

of a parked S.U.V.
rocking steadily, eerily

It takes a moment to see
he's fucking a body

Not male nor female, just thighs
White, hairy, gargantuan thighs

pushed overhead. Suddenly
he backs away a little dazed

Lights a cigarette, staggers into
the street. A moment later

a woman gets out, pulling up
her fuchsia bike shorts. He flicks

his cigarette down the street,
they get back in their seats,

and they're gone.

*

6:30 a.m.

I leave you in bed
to encounter

the grayness, the blue
barely peeking through

A pale mourning dove
shares the moment with me

but looks confused
as it totters on the pilings

This story may end
much sooner than I thought

It may end today
Or every time you think it's over

there'll be something more brutal
left to say. The water is dull

but still magical, and I wonder
Are the gulls *lost*, or is this where

they aim to be? And when did
this become a narrative of

captivity, from what am I trying
to break free? Last night's rain

hangs on all the flowers, I thought
I would watch them through fall

and winter. The pigeons start another
wild wheel, their keeper directing them

from a roof with a tattered
black flag. A whole day

of suffering or civility
headed our way. How did it come

to this, and does it matter? We aim
to be gentle, but end up cruel

That same-old, awful
mystery. My lettuce-colored cup

runs empty.

*

Sweet and Long

Tonight all sorts of ends
shift into view, as
lightning jerks around

the clouds. I could sink
into a certain comfort
here, just disappear

Yet I sense the goddess
gearing up to create
and destroy

with one great arc
of her arm. Just don't
touch me, not yet, or

not here. Something inside
feels broken, a number
that can no longer be

dialed. I have desired
so many times and so many
things, by some law of no

return. But I trust I will live
in my skin again, if life
is sweet and long.

*

Pink Moon

A perfect day at the canal, the sun on my back
healing me, or so I imagined. At sunset two women
took out the red canoe, just paddled around
Later I made you come down and look at the moon
thinking it might heal us, too, with its unbelievable pink
color. Yesterday we found something very hard
at our core, a fierce acorn. I don't know
if we were born with it, or if its mass simply accrued
in the darkness. But I know the moon
has compassion for us. So does the water.

*

Saturday Morning

Last night the world
turned itself
inside-out

with rain, and I hoped
the water today
would be clear

and full. But I
should have
remembered, the rain

always brings in
the sewage. Still
the morning is

gorgeous, a solitary gull
keeps watch over
the water, the current

pulling away
from the harbor. Pale
lavender slicks

move slowly up
the surface, like
horizontal ghosts

The garden has
peaked, the flowers
sagging like hoses

out of their cement
enclosures. Only
the petunias are crawling up

the barbed wire, soon
they will make it over
the top, into the lot

of baby-blue semis,
old orange rowboats
stacked and bound

with yellow rope.
I'm not going to write
about you anymore,

I'm not going to write
to you. I'm not going to write
about anyone. Only

the canal. Over the years
it has been every color—
a glossy black slick,

a greasy chocolate,
a frightening froth
of white and violet.

It has been home to piles
of tires, oil fires, suitcases
full of chopped bodies.

It didn't ask for that,
it didn't ask for
anything. It's not even

angry. It's green, and
has come to live.

*

Summer Song (or, The Rose)

Yesterday a rose burst forth
inside me, today

the rose fled, the world suddenly
colorless. *Your heart*

is breaking, let it
So this is who I always am

Love rushing neither toward
nor away, just a rash muscle quaking

I had forgotten it, perhaps abused it
then I touched it, felt its beat

shaking the walls
Last night I couldn't find my way home again

I walked the streets, tracing the city
in the order it received me

One a.m., two a.m., one apartment
after another, back in Chinatown, invisible again

Then awoke to the rose gone
missing, the boat very dark

You are somewhere swimming
by the breakwater, *breakwater*

coming from your mouth
like the color green itself, laughing

It's time to let go
of this posture, this torque

toward the past
In summer's darkest hour

The heart awakens to what
it already knows, nothing to do

but welcome its raw clarity
Keep a finger on the pulse

The one sound, the one safety.

*

September

I haven't come for
so long. The marigolds

have grown over
the slab, almost nowhere left

to sit. September's brought
a calm purple

flowering, the shadows thick
on the water. The winter is

coming, and I am
leaving. A bird shakes ashes

from its wings, a clump
of red dahlias

lies at the edge, as if
something died here

and it did. A pair of doves
picks at a rusty engine

as the sun illumines
a glut of polliwogs

moving like intelligent, brown
sperm. I honored this place

in my way, and now
it's yours. I don't love you

any less than I did, nor
do I have any more words

to explain why
it's finished. I hosted

a flood here, it changed
my contours

the way only water
can. Once again

the canal has changed
color, to a color

I've never seen—
flaming turquoise streaked

with forest
green. One water,

pulling hard
out to sea.

*

The Real River

Simply put, I didn't know
The current ran so fierce here—

Wake of a yellow water taxi
Orange light disappearing into the west

At the shore of
The bone-strong river

The real river

Hem of the city
Its pale white spire

Kidney burning through one side

Everything speaks
Of its rightness

The salt, the gleam

Rubbing oil onto my hip
Trying to make it better

I lunged at the spot
I thought was wet

Seastreak ferry
Plowing downtown

This is my life now
Utterly jagged by magic

Insert lyricism later

*

Afterword (or, The Bridge)

Because desire always exceeds
its object. Because the energy you gave me

feels big enough to birth wings. Because
I want you to push into the wetness

and I know it. Because of the salt
and the wind. Because everything

that is supposed to happen
will happen, is happening, or

has already happened. Because
ambivalence is more beautiful

than justice. Because my heart is
shooting ahead, and I have no choice

but to follow it. Because I want you
to be happy, with or without me.

Because of the birds fleeing the storm.
Because the harbor is permeable

and shining. Because it felt like
the last night of my life

but it wasn't. Because a web of cables
is there to catch me if I blow

sideways, and always will be. Because
I walked across the bridge and was free.

THE HOSPITAL FOR
SPECIAL CARE

MORNING EN ROUTE TO THE HOSPITAL

Snow wafts off the little lake
along Route 66, momentarily encasing the car

in a trance of glitter

Live with your puny, vulnerable self
Live with her

A HALO OVER THE HOSPITAL

You looked beautiful
Your eyes blue and lucid
Though your face has been reconstructed
by a team of surgeons, just a few little scars
on the bridge of your nose
and under your chin, you'd never know
your skin hung on a rack
and they gave you titanium cheekbones
and a titanium jaw, I couldn't tell either
until I brushed your teeth
trying hard to dislodge the morning's oatmeal
while avoiding the broken ones
Some in the front are apparently little stumps
and inside your gums, an astonishing gnarl of metal
Such miniature machinery! You are truly
a cyborg now, the metal of your jaw linking up
with the metal of your cheekbones, behind the scenes
Now your skull is literally shining. And your arms
can move much more than I thought, and your grace
is utterly intact. But your mouth gets so dry,
I have to trace your delicate lips
with a finger laden with balm, cherry balm
from a tube, make sure my hands are clean
then reapply, reapply. And give you water
from a miniature green sponge on a stick,
a little lollipop of water. *This is*
an incredibly inefficient means of drinking
you observe, and indeed each suck gives you
only a thimbleful. So we have to perform
the feat thousands of times
Try going in through the left side, you advise
and I straddle your bed to do so, trying

to avoid your broken tooth in the front
Just shove it right back in there, you tell me, always
the mentor, always encouraging me
to get it right, to use an adequate angle
and thrust. When you sleep I make sure
you stay breathing, make sure I'm there
when you open your eyes, as you're slightly stricken
upon remembering the prison
your body has become. *I'm frightened*, you say
Then *I'm sad, so sad to be paralyzed*, and I'm sad too
You can't wipe away your tears because your hands
don't move, and I can't wipe them away either
because it's too abrupt a motion, everything now
needs to happen very slowly. So we place
a wet towel across your eyes and the tears
must soak upwards. More ice, more ice, the water
on the little green sponge has to be cold, not
lukewarm, and your fingertips can't touch
the sheet, it's too painful to touch something smooth
OK we'll try propping your hands up
on rough white towels, is that better, yes
You say my hand feels good touching yours
and it's like I won the lottery. You fall asleep again
and I hold your hand, but don't know where
to put my head, so I lay it on your bed beside your hips
and fall asleep too. It's Sunday afternoon. Outside
in the common room there are people
we once might have pitied but now we envy—
double-knee replacement, one amputated arm, big deal
Later I get to wheel you outside, it takes forever
to lift you into the chair and requires a motorized
yellow crane, your body like a beautiful tan bird
in its beak. I try to wheel you slowly like Nurse Peggy said
Slowly down the glass hallways, careful not to raise

your blood pressure, we can go out into the autumn air
but we can't go down to the pond, not yet, you say
you want to see the trees with the gold leaves and so
we do, the leaves fallen along the pathway bunch up
in the wheels of the chair and I get a little panicked,
how do you work this thing, where are the brakes?
Everyone at home wants to know if you are OK
You're not "OK," you're paralyzed and in tremendous pain
Everyone keeps asking, *Do you think she will walk again?*
But that really isn't the issue, the issue today
is your distended stomach, your painful little balloon of gas
Apparently the spine runs the bowels and the blood
and just about everything else, miraculous and hurt
jelly cord. Your whole body suddenly withered and transparent
We can see your muscles move with the electrodes on
You have some tricep, no bicep, your left quad jerked
but no luck on the right, someday you'll recover, I just know it
and I tell you so, I can't stop smoothing your hair, its
blonde laced with gray, growing longer
than it's ever been, and your body
I always wanted to see naked, now
I've seen it twice: once in a photo album
I stumbled upon, photos of you and your lover
naked in your kitchen, you both looked
happy and free, and I felt happy for you
and now here, the aureole of your immobile breast
magnanimous and wide, your legs quiet
and hairy, so not-moving. We discover
some stitches in your calf, someone at the ICU
must have forgotten about them, the nurse pushes on them
and pus comes out, we all wince. They have to come out soon
and so they do. Dinner wheels in, puréed tuna melt, puréed
Black Forest cake, and I imagine this gigantic medieval kitchen
where they make each dish then send it

to an enormous blender and out comes
this ridiculous beige & gray paste. Of course
you're not hungry, the lemon yogurt I fed you
so assiduously in the morning has caused you
unthinkable pain, and to think I pushed you into
eating all of it, agony. I read you an essay of mine
about troubling the passage from the particular to the universal
and you say yes, Maggie, the problem now is to think
the singular. The singular, you say again, very seriously
as if it's ten years prior and we're just sitting in your office
This whole situation is seeming very singular, there's a book
you want me to read but you can't remember the title
so we have to call J, I hold the phone up to your ear
Press it harder, you say, OK, it's called PROVINCIALIZING EUROPE
and I promise to read it, at this point
I'd eat a copy of MEIN KAMPF if you asked me to
I am so sad to be paralyzed
The problem now is to think the singular
The pain is returning and thank God Nurse Winnie
is back on duty, I'm so glad she's curious and presses you
to be articulate, even when you're tired and don't feel like it
She needs more of a description, she doesn't want
you to get an infection, finally you say *Winnie, the pain*
in my intestine is coming from my unconscious, a line
that brings me unending happiness. Later I sit on the bed
and tell you a little about my spastic love life, about the person
I am trying not to be in love with
You ask if we went home and fucked, I say we did
and you are happy, and I love the way the word *Fuck*
comes out of your wired mouth, as if desire can never be
closed down or tortured out, as if *Fuck* will always bubble out
of a metal forest. I tell you a little more
and you say, *Good for fucking, bad for future planning*
You say I don't have to be ashamed of my desire

SOMETHING BRIGHT, THEN HOLES

Not for sex, not for language
You say you've learned by age fifty
that you need them both, together, and that you and J
have that. You've been so happy. Crying now you say
All I can think is that if we built it once
we can build it again and I know you will and tell you so, then kiss
your forehead, the one part of your body
that hasn't sustained any damage
Not one single scratch on your helmet
You took the whole fucking fall
on your chin, the snap back of your head
caused the fracture, the space that's injured
is no bigger than a chocolate bar and yet
here we are. Jelly cord swollen with broken blood
vessels, thousands of nerve cells fighting for life
"Scars form, further distorting any surviving nerve pathways"
"One axon after another turns into a severed stump"
Fuck science, it's so moralistic, and the terrible sensations mean
you will heal because you can feel, like when the nurse
pushed on your stitches until they oozed and you said *Ow*
or when the smoothness of the sheet assails your fingertips
or when you say everything, absolutely everything
feels so tired and sore. Every word a chore, and yet
you give me so many, we discuss direct service
vs. community organizing, your care for the world
simply astonishing. You even make your physical therapist
feel beautiful, by expounding on the virtues
of her new haircut. *Well my husband really likes it*, she says
and you don't even cringe. You change the subject, tell us
the story of your first dog, whose name was
Shameless Hussy. I am happy to see so many competent people
buzzing around your body, I get angry when they move you
too quickly, I like it when they tend to you
tenderly, your head kind of tacked on by a brace

I hate this thing, you say, *but I'm so terrified*
to have it come off, because you know you can't hold
your own head up, it's like being an infant again
but you have all this rich language. And when
they take it off to stretch your head
your neck finally appears, beautiful and clammy
and bluish, a little like the plucked skin of a bird
You ask me to lift your shoulders off the pillow
then set them back down, I try to get the rolled towel
behind your head with one hand while I redistribute
the gelatin of the pillow with the other, *Be a little bolder*, you say
What feels right to you keeps changing
Thousands of times I moisten your mouth with balm
and water. At lights out I drive back to your house
where I sleep on the floor of your office, amidst
the hundreds of projects you left in-progress
Piles of books and papers, tracts about
global feminism, calls for social justice
I cry a little then, in mourning for
your graceful and butch handwriting
But I know now where you are, and where you will be
for some time, gold leaves swirling outside
your window, gold leaves making a halo
A halo over the hospital

AT THE HOSPITAL FOR SPECIAL CARE

O this dome of sadness

How to be a pupil placed
in it, be a pupil of it

Today I will learn how to hoist her onto the board

*

I go to tumble-dry the blankets so they'll be warm
when we wrap your hands, say hi to the man who has none

He's watching *The Bold and the Beautiful* at maximum volume
in the common room, a Sears Catalogue and Blood Glucose Diary

inert in his lap. Soon you will wake up with your brow
furrowed, say, *I was sleeping.* Yes, I'll say, you were.

Then a little later, *I was in a terrible accident.*
Yes, I'll say again. You were.

*

By her bed
The pain makes her gray

Lips coming off in strips
The fight to keep her teeth from decay

Arjo, Oscar Boots
The new words for today

*

You hate the holiday décor, it's obtrusive
and aggressively secular—

Cut-outs of manic snowmen, oversized
peppermint patties made of Styrofoam.

A nurse offers me a sugar cookie shaped
like a pine tree, heavy with green icing

while I wait for them to finish your bowel routine.
The American Movie Channel is showing a Western—

hot brunette in a nightshirt, blue ribbons, big tits,
some cattle swimming across a river. The nurses sit

in a circle, picking at the cookies, complaining—justly—
about their hours, while Celine Dion wonders

Why can't it feel like Christmas all the time
on the hallway speakers.

*

Exiled to the common room while they wash her

Just me and the guy with stumps. He asks Nurse Marta
for a glass of water, Marta who is so happy

because her son is finally moving in
with his girlfriend. *It's a start*, she winks at us.

The man with stumps says nothing, leans forward
to itch his head on the table, then takes a long drink

of water, from the longest straw

*

This is my favorite time here—
you asleep, me keeping watch.

Making sure of the dusk.

In the low light I try to make out
the notes posted on pastel paper:

SOFT COLLAR IN BED ONLY. PURÉE DIET.
TURN HEAD AND TRUNK TOGETHER.

Outside: two birds at the feeder.

*

She says she'll shoot herself if she's in this kind of pain tomorrow
All I can think to say is, *Luckily we don't have the utensils for that kind of thing in here*

I can't make her smile, I miss her
good color, her happiness

She calls her mouth a trainwreck
I stare at the trumpet of white and red amaryllis

No machetes here, no international villains
No chartable march toward health or death

Just the eternal present of a single body
being driven insane by pointless pain

In this dead air place
She still breathes

SOMETHING BRIGHT,
THEN HOLES

THE MUTE STORY OF NOVEMBER

Living as if every moment announced a beloved
and it does

Then the bleeding-off

Maybe you are the sea to me, or me to you
A reasonable enough supposition

Can't you see, I'm busy
triangulating

Gingko leaves at my feet
A flood of questing yellow

They say that everything that is growing
will stop growing soon, maybe

this weekend, the first deep freeze
The season of falling

will give way to the season
of brittle upturned sticks

Who cares, it's all equally gorgeous
and last night, a lunar eclipse

Immaculate white moving in and out
of a rusty red rind, I pulled

a sheet of Plexiglas over
the hole in the roof

so I could watch it from inside the boat
The boat from which we ride the sky

Nothing can go wrong, do you understand
Nothing can ever go wrong

This is what happens when you cease
your management

The blue and gold of the morning
just appear on the sidewalk, ongoing drift

of garbage, a tire is good to sit in
A window pane may flake in the wind

The mute story of November

I don't even have to steal
your words, you give them to me for free

So strange to know that you can and cannot hurt me
My heart just can't break any more, now that

it has changed substance, is full
of fluid and fire and air and turning

like a little wheel in its broth

And I can and cannot hurt you either, now that
I am utterly virginal, preposterous

as that may sound, it's also true
Sometimes you get to start anew

The pages of my book wet and limpid
with tea, on a Sunday, the spidery plants

reaching haphazardly in all directions
from their dilapidated mobile, it's part

of the magic here, and the painted green
cement floor. *What part of this autonomy*

am I not supposed to like?; I too have been
much lonelier. Maybe in eleven rooms

you'll find some sort of home, or base, it's like
there's this enormous surplus of feelings and/or words

and we prick at the tarp, letting little pinwheels of light come in
but never really touching the source

So little time, really, we've eaten some food, slept badly
swam in jumbled waters, very little coming

I don't even know you, shadowed by the knowing
The knowing that has nothing to do

with life-stories, their wicked specificity
Sometimes my speech moves so fast inside me

before it hatches, and I know I'm about to flop over
into tongues, but I don't care: this is the speed

at which I run, and you run fast, too, so I let you
touch me with one hand while the other steers a car

through midtown Manhattan, it's almost as if
none of this has ever happened, it just shines

then gets enclosed in an envelope decorated with faded blue stamps
from the Belgian Congo. It's such a relief

when tears come from the cold, like yesterday
on River Street, all the men lined up in their idling cars

by the power plant, what are they waiting for?
With all due humility, I have to say

I know it now, or it knows me
the peace-feeling

that stays even as the body races and pants
above or along it, when the team suddenly does

a jazz square in unison, when a dream repeals
an impediment overnight, when the whole world

The whole world is strobing

MERCURIAL

I have been warned
against you. *Mercurial*

one friend says, and
I wonder, Is mercury

a form of blue? When or where
does silver break

into blue? Or forget, if you can,
about color: it's about

how it moves. And I am
quick, changeable

Close to the sun, too

INTERLUDE

punctured into the real
by a thumb

in the throat, making
presence

the only possible

your skin a friend
I am getting to know

in intervals

OUR JOB

I love the crazy look you get at night
when you think there might be rats nearby

Yet in the morning I come home and cry, thinking
like Spock: *This feeling has all the characteristics of pain*

Look at you, someone says; who, then, does
the looking? I hate the phrase "self-preservation"

I mean what, exactly, is one
preserving? Then I remember

about GUARD RAILS, GUARD RAILS
FOR THE HEART, how did I miss

that one? It's all because
I'm an ectomorph, and you are too

"Lean and slightly muscular"
It's our job, you say, our job to feel

Our job
to see it through

EVERYONE NEEDS

A bubble in the blood
that lodged years earlier
finds its way up and out

My mouth opens to give you
its flower of froth
You roll down the window

to receive it, very
smooth. Now do I have to be
haunted by the bumblebee

atop my burgundy
ficus, do I have to imagine
your emissions, a fire trail

hosting the sun
Everyone needs an ocean
Everyone needs to pray

at its mean, black lap.

PROMISE

You promise me nothing

I distract myself from this fact
by wondering about the etymology

of *promise*, promise myself
to look it up later

For now there is a home here

In this bent head
This hand in hair

THANKSGIVING

Can beauty save us? Yesterday
I looked at the river and a sliver
of moon and knew the answer;

today I fell asleep in a spot of sun
behind a Vermont barn, woke to
darkness, a thin whistle of wind

and the answer changed. Inside the barn
the boys build bongs out of
copper piping, electrical tape, and

jars. All of the children here have
leaky brown eyes, and a certain precision
of gesture. Even the maple syrup

tastes like liquor. After dinner
I sit the cutest little boy on my knee
and read him a book about the history of cod

absentmindedly explaining overfishing,
the slave trade. *People for rum?* he asks,
incredulously. *Yes,* I nod. *People for rum.*

WHAT IT IS

It is what
it is. But
what is it?

What it is—

Some soft
tautology

whose two terms
are touch

Time to give, time
to give it up.

ON THE DAY OF YOUR LEAVE-TAKING

On the day of your leave-taking
I wouldn't want to see you anyway
I want to be alone with my vagrant ugliness
Want the bridge suddenly to double its span
so the only parameter becomes the vanishing
of my already thin-soled shoes
On a Friday night, one girl hangs from a trapeze by her shins
You think it looks scary but having lived among them
I know there's always a safety (in this case, the toes)
Another girl enjoys bars with themes
Another is painting bunnies in Kentucky
I am taking my welts to the tub
hoping the porcelain is free of blood and hair
The blood and hair I left there, streaking
the pale pink soap melting into the brick wall
which grows black and green with companions
People continue to grind the veiny fat into the asphalt
with their feet, it's only nine degrees, my river rocks
now bearded with ice. So the fat freezes and a spoon
wedged into the cement glistens, I keep wanting
to pick up every hard and bright object I find
and put it in a Mason jar, then add blue pigment
and shake. Gnarled hand of green glass, leftover
confetti, petrified pieces of pizza that appear
near the trio of homeless men who watch a shaky TV
hooked into a generator in a parking lot, it's where
I get my news these days and why not, they always
know the score, the five-day weather report. I can see you
boarding your jet plane, see you with your hat on crooked
as if you recently tumbled onto the planet out of the carapace
of a rumpled goddess. I hear the gulf is a little bellicose
but beyond that, livable, despite the depressing stats
from that part of the world, and you know I'll be here, perched
into blotchy corners, not knowing what life
could possibly mean without its soundtrack

so I can hum along to its pain, as if its humdrum
or shared nature could possibly dim its particular
luster. But it's the cold that makes my mascara pool up
around my eyes and gives a shock to my quads
as they push forward, the only idiot crossing the bridge
at sunset, but you have to march across the span
while you can, before winter's sweet cocoon
gets punctured and happiness presents itself
as an option, and I have to accept the possibility
of another body in my bed. I keep dreaming it's
someone else that's paralyzed, a childhood friend
I've fallen out of touch with, I keep dreaming
we're fucking but somehow never alone, sometimes
I think it would be so hot to fuck you with another
and other times I know I'm just making the best
of a bad situation. Have I mentioned I'm watching
a man softly cry as he searches for a lost pill
under the pillows of a sage-colored couch, he has
a cough that comes from the Underworld, one lens
of his glasses dramatically cracked. I want
to hold him, the way I want to hold anyone
who seems contagious. Maybe we could
keep each other warm. And you emptied yourself
twice into my throat and I remain utterly starved
for more, the smell of one sex intimating the smell of another
but who am I kidding, really, on this January day
that has dwindled into the single digits, in which
we have to pin the drapes shut with safety pins
and stuff towels into the honeycombed walls
I just want to be called out as the greedy whore that I am

LANDSCAPE

Men in yellow slickers
high up on ladders
washing the brick

Brick-colored water
flooding the gutters
Thick rivulets of brick

The timing is off, I think you understand
I will never understand
I will live forever

in this hexagon
of non-understanding
Nailed to it, its redness

WINTER SONG

Solitude is a gift
Say it to yourself
under a canopy
of phony stars

Think of Lily in
her old season, living
with three pale cats
Her mind a lavender wash

Think of the man floating spray mums
at the feet of the colossus
before a day spent staring
at the wall

On the great ceiling of plates
and grates, a single leaf scrapes by
as the clear poison singes its path
from nostril to deep brain

The winter is not too sad, say it
then sing it
from your new pod, your new fig
made of glass

TRIOLET

The cut on my mouth was shaped like a country;
I showed it to you and you ran into the trees.
Maybe the trees needed you, or maybe you needed the trees.
The cut on my mouth was shaped like a country;
it bled until the rain said, *That's enough*. It bled
until the rain said, *That's enough now*. It bled,
the cut on my mouth shaped like a country;
I showed it to you and you ran into the trees.

TELL ME

You are gone now, truly
and to look you up in the dictionary
is no longer possible or

enough. The new season's arrow
cleaves the maudlin
right out of the air, stays

the wavering knife. *Better off*
without you, say the crickets, say
the Christmas tree lights

which each night make a party
out of the darkness, tell me
which green porch is home.

THE ROSE

And who wouldn't hate
all the poor, suffering mothers
sick with their eros and wine

I hate them all, hate her, too
and do not recall
any early drenching

in good-smelling fabrics, no
big-mouthed flowers, no
free-flowing food. So

to stand here and be pierced
To be pierced by her breath
breathing through my body

O inevitable, changeable rose.

FATHER'S DAY

Alone at last
with this damp pain
with which I came

into being
Who knows what I am
beyond it, beyond

its unease
The air is still
There is no breeze

No wind to strip me
into petals. If you
were to reappear now

we could lay our losses
side-by-side, two gifts
the ocean dragged in

One a tentacle longer
than the other, both
raucously unhealed. As it is

there ought to be a law
against this loneliness,
the kind you brought

without meaning it.
I remember when
my first love said, *If it hurts*

so bad, why not just dull it
with a sharp object? Now
I dream it—a blade

racing through skin
then organ, blood flooding
round the incision, no

suction, no cup
No rags, no mop
Nothing on earth

to make it stop.
Grief shines a light
as well as a dark.

I ask you, how much
can a person change
in one lifetime? You say

Hurry, hurry.

A RETURN

You came to salt the earth
and you salted it.

I came on my heel.

You lifted our shirt flaps and instructed
skin and scar

to talk, baby cheeks hot
with fever. They talked.

I came on my heel.

You came to salt the earth
and you salted it, but I was too tired of mourning

to mourn any more.
Lie: I mourned a little more.

I came on my heel.

You came on my belly, in my mouth,
near my mouth, then on my belly again.

Inside I was pink with ants, very happy
ants. You felt it. I was glad.

I revisited my despair and found myself
used to it. No triumph there.

Not fair. Salted.

MORNING PRAYERS

1.

This morning I awoke with a fresh sense
of total, desperate hell

Our failure to love each other well

O let a jesus come down and make it sweet
Let a jesus take an axe to the wheel

Part the fire with tongs

2. (How not to fall)

You close your eyes and say *waves*
Yes, everything happens now in waves

I wanted to pull an okayness over me
so I lied about longing

Lied in the morning, then lied
in the evening

Then dropped the smallest granules into
a glass capsule, just trying to stay close

to the slope's soil

3. (Radio Play)

Auroras are not definite until they happen
In fact the cards are always stacked against a good aurora

The sweet word hasn't worn off
It's just worn

Stop shaking the wound

If you want to see something glorious
Look at the Pleiades

4. (Something bright)

We share a brightness
It's called death
in life

I toss and turn all night, hearing you say
I want to touch you
without using my hands

Then wake up with an offer:
The hype of my clarity
My good clench and ache

5. (Then holes)

Every morning the shadow of my hand haunts
this table, asking, *Can I bleed
here, can I become free here*

*Don't want to be free
want to be with you,* says the monster
But he is literally

a monster. And I seek
a different life, one
of constant rapture

though I know the shadow will soon return
with new questions, like
Is this theater?

6. (The Cinema)

And I beat myself
here, hoisted myself
onto this cliff

Blindfolded girl
in a party dress
poised at the edge

Ready to slake
the village appetite
for sacrifice

O begin again, begin
again.

7. (Athens)

After reading about a girl who was killed
by a knife-wound straight through to
a ventricle of her heart, I took a walk
in the rural cemetery. There I saw
two dead birds: one a scrawny baby; the other
fat, gray-feathered. Both equally dead, though
one was ringed with ants, the other
fresher. At the end of the path lay
a field, home to a regal, light-brown mare
and her foal. It was there
that I said a prayer
to the brown and blue notebooks
of your arms.

ACKNOWLEDGMENTS

Grateful acknowledgment to the editors of the following publications, in which versions of some of these poems first appeared: *belladonna*Books* #42, *Black Clock, Fort Necessity, Fugue, Hanging Loose, The Hat, Lyric, Pocket Myths, Tool: A Magazine* and *The Tiny*.

Cover art: "Heartattack City" by Tara Jane O'Neil.

Thefts:

    "something bright and then holes"
       —Marius Von Senden, *Space and Sight*
       as channeled by Annie Dillard

    p. 54: "As if every event/announced a beloved"
       —Rilke, the First Duino Elegy

    p. 76: "Then I began to get terribly hyped on clarity"
       —Diane Arbus's journal, 1973

    p. 77: *"Don't want to be free want to be with you"*
       —Anne Carson, *Autobiography of Red*

Thanks:

    Richard Nash & Soft Skull Press, for their loyalty and vision
    Sarah Kemphaus, for her birds, & the example of her quiet living
    Eileen Myles & Anthony McCann, for wisdom in the final hours.

"The Canal Diaries" is for Brian, who knows it is all one water.
"The Hospital for Special Care" is for Christina, teacher & friend for all time.

The rest is for Nick, *nel mezzo del cammin*.

Maggie Nelson is most recently the author of *The Red Parts* (2007) and *Women, the New York School, and Other True Abstractions* (2007). Her previous books of poetry include *Jane: A Murder* (2005; finalist, the PEN/Martha Albrand Award for the Art of the Memoir), *The Latest Winter* (2003), and *Shiner* (2001). A recipient of a 2007 Creative Capital Arts Writers grant, she currently teaches at CalArts and lives in Los Angeles.

author photo by Tom Atwood